CW01083894

More Muscle More Better.

BUILDING A GREAT MALE PHYSIQUE
USING THE OLD-SCHOOL GOLDEN ERA
BASICS

JACOB HENLEY

NASM - Certified Personal Trainer

MORE MUSCLE MORE BETTER

Copyright © 2022 Jacob Henley

All rights reserved.

ISBN:
9798831808087

DEDICATION

This book could be dedicated to many things, but only one truly matters... a long, happy, and healthy life spent with the ones I love, doing the things I love doing. Investing in my health is the only way I've found to buy time.

For more information and other great reads follow me on my social media platforms listed below:

IG: @realjacobhenley
TW: @realjacobhenley
FB: Jacob Dean Henley

CONTENTS

Not all exercises are suitable for everyone and this or any other exercise program may result in injury. PLEASE ALWAYS consult your DOCTOR before beginning this or any other exercise program, especially if you have any chronic or recurring condition, and/or if you are pregnant, nursing, or elderly. This exercise program is NOT recommended if you experience chest pains or have uncontrolled blood pressure or other uncontrolled chronic diseases. • By performing any of the exercises in this program, you assume ALL risks of injury from doing so. The author, writer, and/or publisher of this book, program, an audio file, video file, digital content, or any other media format is NOT responsible or liable for any injury or loss you may sustain by participating in this exercise program. • ALWAYS warm up before beginning any workout and NEVER exercise beyond the level at which you feel comfortable. • PLEASE stop exercising immediately if you experience pain, soreness, fatigue, shortness of breath, dizziness, lightheadedness, blurred vision, headache, nausea, sickness, illness, dehydration, excessive sweating, or any other discomfort. If any of these symptoms persist after you stop exercising, please seek medical help immediately. • This exercise program and the tutorials and instructions provided in this program are NOT intended, and should NOT be used, as a substitute for professional medical advice, diagnosis, or treatment. • The author, writer, and/or publisher of this book, program, an audio file, video file, digital content, or any other media format or content, make NO representation or warranty, whether expressed or implied, with respect to the safety, usefulness, or the result of this exercise program.

1 THE INTRO

Mmmm muscles. The fleshly substance that makes up the difference between flab and fabulous. For centuries society drilled into our heads that the perfect male body is a chiseled piece of man meat sporting large biceps, yoked quads, and a serious six-pack. This is mostly correct, however, isn't realistically achievable for everyone.

Some people are honestly way too busy to get there, and if that's you, you're in the right place. In this book, I will break down the very basics of strength training, muscle building, and the diets to go along with them.

Now don't get me wrong, you will have all the information you need to achieve a body from Greek mythology, but if that's not you, you can just settle for a moderately fit, toned, tight body, that still rocks harder than all the milkshakes. I will be providing you with two training program options, a 3-day and 5-day to fit even the busiest of all schedules.

My programs are designed for the extremely busy, hustle-busting, nose-grinding guys out there who want to be yoked but are also devoting time to their professional lives that they can't pull away from.

Once you learn the program flow, you'll be able to leave the gym with a dirty sick pump in 45 minutes or less and in just 30 days drastically improve your body's composition.

With less than 100 pages of actual wordage, my goal in writing this book is to break everything down and make it as cheap and easy as possible to understand the basics of health, fitness, and weightlifting. I designed this book to be easy to read and finished in just a few days so you can get started working on the body of your dreams as soon as possible.

I won't be proving you with large amounts of scientific information or long-drawn-out explanations. You're getting only what you need to know to get to where you want to be. I'm a firm believer in self-discovery and self-education so if you want to dive a little deeper, that work is on you, but I have attached all sited research to the back, marked with corresponding site numbers throughout the book.

What This Is Not

This will not be polite, and will probably offend you once or twice. Good. It's designed to hurt.

This is not a cross-training program. Those are effective, work amazing for some people, and will make a man out of you, but they also require an extremely unnecessary amount of exertion that is not suitable for "everyone" despite what their flyer may say.

Look, you just want to burn fat and build muscle like everyone else right? Then why would you want to wear a weighted vest, do 100 burpees, 400 air squats, and pretend like you're doing real pull-ups just to get those results? I understand and respect cross-training is a lifestyle and some people just love it, but for everyone else, it's overkill and will eventually cause them to give up or injured because it's way too demanding if you're not a truly devoted maniac.

This is not a cakewalk, but it is a simplistic "battle-proven" program that just freaking works. No fancy machines, no crazy supplements, and no BS. We're going back to the basics of grit, grind, steel and iron.

This is not meant to be temporary, and if you give it 100% for at least 30 days, I'm sure you'll be so impressed with yourself that it will become a permanent staple to your lifestyle.

First, to make it easier for you to follow along with me, I want to provide you with some definitions and nomenclature you may hear or read about in this new genre of life. I will also walk you through some myths that are just absolute crap and better to go ahead and squash now. Don't let these definitions intimidate you, this industry just likes to use big words and acronyms to explain things. I got you.

Definitions

Fad Diet – A diet that is the latest fad being plastered all over the TV and internet. Keto, caveman, paleo, military, fasting, and the list goes on and on. I have tried all of these diets, and I can tell you first hand... they all actually work.

These diets all work because they are all based on the basic principles of eating less food and burning more calories (being in a calorie deficit). They are still full of over complications, empty promises, and claims that just aren't true, but you're guaranteed to lose weight for a little while.

The diet program I'm giving to you is different because it's balanced, full of normal food, and sustainable. You'll be eating regular foods, still able to go to restaurants, and still be able to party with your friends. It's not a crazy fad, It's just eating like you got some, dare I say, common sense.

Calorie – a calorie is the unit of measurement which represents the amount of energy (heat) required to raise 1 kilogram (kg) of water 1° Celsius (C). Converted that's 1 liter (or 34 fl. Oz.) of water raised 33.8° Fahrenheit (f).

Macronutrients – The large portions of a diet's nutritional breakdown. Proteins, carbohydrates (carbs), and fats. These are also the nutrients that provide 99% of a food's calories. There are 4 calories in 1 gram of protein, 4 calories per 1 gram of carbs, and 9 calories per gram of fat.

Micronutrients – The small portions of a diet's nutritional breakdown. Vitamins and minerals. There are no calorie representations for micronutrients.

Amino Acids – In school, you probably learned that amino acids were the building blocks of protein, but did you know there are 20 of them? There are 2 types you will hear about most often in the weightlifting world, branched-chain amino acids (BCAAs), and essential amino acids (EAAs).
    BCAA – Can be created by the body
    EAA – Cannot be created by the body, must be consumed by either food or supplementation.

These will most often be pitched as supplements necessary for muscle growth. The supplements aren't required, but the amino acids are. A well-balanced diet will contain all the amino acids you need, so no need to buy the supplement in my opinion.

Glycogen – Your body stores the carbs you ingest as glycogen inside the liver and muscles. It is the body's most readily available and preferred energy source. Some diets claim you can convert your body over to burn fat instead of glycogen, but that's not *entirely* true and involves a super low carb diet. We won't be doing that in this program, carbs are not the enemy, indulgence is the enemy.

Fiber – The weird and hard-to-understand uncle of the nutrition family. Fiber isn't digested like everything else, some professionals say it's not digested at all. Technically dumbed a type of carbohydrate, and comes in 2 forms, insoluble and soluble.

Insoluble fiber comes from eating fruit skins, veggies, nuts, and wheat. It cannot be digested through normal means inside humans. Commonly referred to as roughage to keep your bowel movements more regular.

Soluble fiber comes from things like beans, the inside portion of fruit, and even some jams and gums. Turns into a gel-like substance in the body and slows down digestion, giving a better blood sugar response and leaving you feeling more satiated.

Net Carbs – Unless you've been living under a rock for the past few years, you've probably heard of *net carbs*. This term was born from fiber's stubborn inappropriate behavior.

Take the number of carbs, subtract the amount of fiber, and you're left with **net carbs**.

For example, if a whole-wheat cracker has 10 grams of carbs, and 2 grams of fiber, according to the rules of net carbs, it only has 8 carbs. This is allegedly because your body doesn't digest fiber. Or does it?

Just because your body doesn't have the proper enzymes to digest fiber like it does everything else, doesn't me it's not breaking it down and utilizing it. Fiber is still broken down and utilized in the body through a process of internal fermentation.

Your body has a microbiome system (small living organisms) living inside of it that ferments fiber and converts it to a short-chain fatty acid that your body then uses for energy... just like it uses glycogen. That sounds a lot like digestion to me, however, I will yield to the fact that this would have little to no effect on your blood sugar or insulin levels thus potentially being an empty calorie/nutrient. There simply is not enough data for a firm stance in either direction.

Now you really don't need to know any of that for this program, but now you know what to tell people chasing fad diets when you mention to them that *this program doesn't* use that silly net carb mumbo jumbo. I have explained it to you just so you can forget about it. Count the carbs on the back of the freaking box and call it done. Don't make things more complicated.

Simple Carbohydrates – White carbs and sugars that are absorbed by the body faster than complex brown carbs. Good to use if your need a quick meal before or after a workout for faster nutrition absorption.

Complex Carbohydrates – Brown, whole grains, and the carbs found in vegetables. Slower digesting than simple carbs. Normally have more nutrients and fiber than simple carbs.

Hypertrophy – The process of causing micro-tears in a muscle through weightlifting, then having that muscle heal, rebuild, and recover bigger than it was before. Doing this over and over again is how you go from "Buddy" to Studdy.

This constant state of healing and recovering is the reason fitness programs always insist on a good diet. Not only for health and weight loss, but also muscles that are healing need proper nutrition.

Skinny Fat – What you get when someone is skinny, or perhaps underweight, but still has "man boobs" and a flabby body. What this person lacks is muscle mass and calories. Even some distance runners can be skinny fat, as running too much without replenishing those calories, can drastically reduce your muscle mass.

BMI – Body Mass Index – a person's weight in kilograms divided by the square of their height in meters equals their BMI.

A very basic body composition formula to determine a person's weight category. Is not always an accurate representation of someone's fitness level as you can be 185 lbs., 10% body fat, 5'5", and somehow be considered overweight. If you don't already know, 10% at 185 lbs. is not overweight, it's spectacular.

Even though it can be completely bogus, knowing your BMI will help track changes in your body.

BMR – Basal Metabolic Rate – The number of calories (energy/heat) it takes to keep your body alive and functioning at rest. Meaning the amount of energy your body would use if you were just lying in bed all day doing nothing but the automatic bodily functions such as breathing, circulating blood, digesting, etc.

TDEE – Total Daily Energy Expenditure – The total amount of energy you use (calories you burn) during the typical day. This will be a combination of your BMR plus your daily activities like walking to work, working out, washing the dogs, etc.

Working Weight – The phrase we will use to represent the weight you are using in your actual working sets (non-warm-up sets). This weight will change as you get stronger.

Rep(s) – Repetition(s) – is used to count the number of times your lift something. If you curl a dumbbell 4 times, that's 4 *reps*.

Sets – The number of times you do an exercise between resting periods. If you curl a dumbbell 4 reps, rest 1 minute and then curl it 4 more reps, you have performed 2 *sets*.

Superset – Supersets are when you do one set of multiple exercises back to back without resting in between. For example, 1 set of crunches followed by 1 set of leg raises followed by 1 set of mountain climbers, with no rest in between.

Supersets can be a lot of unnecessary strain on the muscle, so this program doesn't call for them often. You will see them for abdominal, tricep, and calf workouts because those muscle groups are stubborn and will need it.

Drop Set – When you do multiple sets of the same exercise, dropping in weight every set, with no rest in between.

For example, barbell curls start at 95 lbs. for 1 set, drop to 85 lbs. for 1 set, and end on 75 lbs. for 1 final set.

This program won't call for any of these, but It's something you should know about to communicate with other fellow gym-goers

Spot – If you go to a public gym more than twice in your life, someone is bound to ask you for a "spot" or a "Spotty Wotty" if you will.

A spot is simply when someone moves in closer to another person who is performing a lift, such as the bench press or squat, and stands there just in case the lift goes astray.

Your job is then to assist the bar up/off or help them guide it safely to the rack. Do *NOT* touch the bar until a spot is requested by some sort of loud grunting communication. Make them work for it, but don't wait once it's called for.

You should not need a spot on every lift when you're operating at normal levels. No one likes the guy who asks for a spot every single time. If you're going for a personal record in weight or reps or nursing an injury, yeah sure, but don't push it. Don't lift more than you can handle on your own.

Remember to always discuss what the lifter expects from the spotter before lifting copious amounts of weight.

Lift Off – The same homie who asked you for a spot may ask you for a lift-off. Most commonly requested on the bench press. This simply means help them lift it off the rack, into position, and then move your hands out of the way.

P.R. – Short for Personal Record. If someone says they broke a P.R. that means they broke a personal record in either weight or reps and are now expecting a high-five.

Hard Gainer – Something someone calls themselves when they're trying to bulk up but can't seem to gain weight. These are three types of people here, 1. A genuine medical condition. 2. Lazy not eating enough, not working out hard enough. 3. Doing too much cardio and not replenishing enough calories. If you think you're a hard gainer... you're probably not.

Myths

Myth No 1. Cardio is king – No, it is not. Cardio is good for you, yes, but when done alone, cardio can actually decrease muscle mass[9]. Why lose weight if you're just going to have less muscle mass? We want balance. A proper cardio regiment will be explained in chapter 4.

Myth No 2. Lifting weights makes you too bulky – This is a fear mostly formed in females, but I understand it may be a concern for some males as well.

This will tighten your skin, improve your life, and increase your lean muscle mass but that doesn't always mean "bulky". Lift weights, avoid eating like a truck driver, get some cardio in, and I promise you'll be happy with the way you look. Don't chase being skinny, chase being "lean".

It has everything to do with how you eat. If you don't want to look bulky, don't choose the bulking diet plan, choose a cutting or maintaining plan instead (all provided later).

Myth No 3. Everyone who doesn't look as crappy as I do is on steroids – The guy on your TV, yeah most likely on roids. The guy in the gym working his butt off out lifting you, probably not. Most guys with great bodies are just normal guys with great bodies.

I hate to tell you this, but even if he is on steroids, he was probably outworking you long before he started taking them. Steroids don't make things easier, but they do make things more possible. It still requires hard work, dedication, and a lot of calories.

Where steroids start to change things is when you feel like you can't go another rep, he can find two more reps and 5 more lbs., but I assure you those last two reps are still heavy and still hurt. They also heal and recover faster.

As a non-steroid user, your genetic potential may cap at a 400 lbs. squat, while Roid-Man's squat reached its cap a long time ago but he shattered the glass ceiling. Yes, he used pills and drugs to do that, but he also used reps, sets, and calories.

I do not recommend steroids outside of doctor's care and suggest you never take them, however, don't use someone else's drug abuse as an excuse for why you probably suck. You're probably one of those grown men who prefer to eat plain cheese pizza over meat lovers.

Myth No. 4 The body can only digest 30 grams of protein at a time – If I had a dollar for every time someone saw me eating one of my meal preps telling me I was overeating protein because the body can only digest 30 grams per hour, I would have a lot of dollars.

These people were always either weak, small, and/or very out of shape. They were also wrong. I didn't bother trying to argue with them, as eating my meal was way more important at the time.

Let's say you eat 60 grams of protein in one sitting, twice the amount of the all-holy number 30. 1 hour goes by and your body effectively digests and utilizes 30 grams... so now what? According to them, your body is just done with it? Sorry, but no.

After you chew it, food takes about six to eight hours to move through your stomach and small intestine, but it doesn't stop there. Food then enters your large intestine (colon) for further digestion, still absorbing water and nutrients. It then finally enters the elimination period (poop). In total it takes about 36 hours for food to move through the entire colon. It is digesting and absorbing nutrients that entire time.

I hope we can all feel better now knowing your body doesn't just randomly stop digesting/absorbing nutrients after 30 minutes.

Myth No. 5 I must change my routine and confuse my muscles to keep them growing – No. Number 1 reason NOT to switch? Switching up your routine prevents you from properly tracking and evaluating your progress. We need organized consistency. Switching your program up and having to find your groove all over again will only slow you down and take time away from you.

There is no cognitive behavior in the muscle, so confusing it can be thrown out of the window too.

What do you do when your lifts get easy? Add more freaking weight. More weight promotes more hypertrophy, builds more muscle, and muscle burns fat. I am science.

Myth No. 6 Increased reps and increased sets equal increased muscle – Also no. Muscles have to be rested and fed. It's as simple as that. Allowing them to recover and proving them with enough food to grow is the ONLY way they'll grow. They can be over trained.

I'm not only talking about rest days either. Rest between sets is equally important. If you try to squeeze out a few more reps on a set just because it feels good, your form will probably go to crap and there's a good chance you'll be doing fewer reps on your next set all together. This program will have you resting 2-3 minutes between each set to prime the muscle for more smooth, controlled, heavy sets to follow.

Myths No. 7 Diet soda is the Devil.
This has been debunked for a long time now thanks to newer randomized controlled human trials. The old studies that were done on lab rats had high doses of the isolated compound (artificial sweeteners) and were nowhere close to accurate "scaled" representations of the amounts humans are consuming from diet sodas and other zero calories beverages.[1]

Some people also say that artificial sweeteners can harm healthy gut bacteria and make you fat, but those studies were again isolated compounds applied directly to cells in a petri dish. That same study was done in a randomized controlled human trial and found little to no change at all. [2]

The fewer chemicals you put in your body the better, but diet coke is not making you fat, isn't killing you[3], and is not the Devil. You're fat from overeating and not moving.

Myths No. 8 through Infinity – Creatine
I could write a whole chapter on creatine myths and why they're all crap. Here are a few of the more popular myths

that the local *Socks-With-Flops-Wearers* in your gym will probably throw around.

Creatine will make you fat – It will not make you fat. You will hold more water for about a week or two, but so long as you properly hydrate every day, your body will even itself back out and you'll soon reap all the benefits of using creatine without the little bit of water retention.

Creatine is bad for your kidneys – This has been proven false many times now. Creatine is now the most studied workout supplement in the world, you can rest easy. So long as you are properly hydrated, and not suffering from any preexisting conditions, then you're good to go. [4]

Creatine will cause Rhabdomyolysis and dehydration – Creatine pulls water into the muscle and keeps it saturated. Unless you have a preexisting condition, drink water and stay hydrated like you're supposed to and you'll be fine. Rhabdo can happen to anyone who isn't properly hydrated and undergoing physical activity. [4]

Creatine is like a steroid – Don't even. It's actually a combination of 3 amino acids (L-arginine, glycine, and L-methionine). Creatine is naturally occurring in your body right now. Your body makes it, uses it, and you ingest it went you consume meat and fish.

You don't need creatine – Yes you do. You may not need to supplement with it, but your body does indeed need it to supply energy to your cells, specifically your muscle cells.

2 PROGRAM BRIEFING

Muscle building and strength training go hand and hand but remember they are two different things and are trained in different ways. We want both of them perfectly calibrated to balance the scales of being really, really good-looking and strong AF. To do that you need a finely tuned ratio of reps-to-weight that I will go over later in this book. We'll start by explaining how to build muscle.

How Do You Build Muscle?

When you properly lift weights you are causing small tears in your muscle fibers (this is one reason you're sore the next few days). Tearing those muscles, allowing them to recover, and providing them with proper nutrients, will heal the little tears and bring them back a little bit bigger. Repeating this over and over again can cause visible growth in as little as one month.

The program style we are going to be doing is called Progressive Muscle Overloading (PMO). This means break down the muscle by strategically overloading it (causing those micro-tears), allowing it to recover, providing it with adequate nutrition, and overloading it again with just a little more weight than last time.

Why Lift Weights When I Can Just Diet?

There are multiple benefits to building muscle. The most popular benefit, it burns fat. Yes, building muscle burns, and rearranges fat in your body! Have you ever known someone who is a "skinny" person but is still a little soft, and flabby? This is called skinny fat and this is what happens when you're skinny in stature but don't eat right and don't do anything to build muscle. That person lacks muscle mass, lacks nutrients, and probably keeps crashing their metabolic system (the way your body uses food for energy).

Other benefits of muscle building include healthier hormonal regulation, increased longevity of life, increased strength, increased stamina, better sleep, improved blood sugar and blood pressure, bone density, flexibility, stronger joints, reduces the likelihood of falls, improves mental health, and increased self-confidence just to name a few. [16]

It should be noted that these benefits go hand and hand with a good diet. I'll be going over a simple, clean, delicious diet later in the book.

Results and Fear of Results

Adding muscle to your frame will also add weight. You may feel kind of strange one day when you love what you see in the mirror, but don't like what you see on the scale. It's okay, don't freak out.

Muscle weighs more than fat, and weightlifting with a proper diet will also increase the density/weight of your bones. You will probably weigh a little more, and there's no way of getting around it. This is the difference between being lean, and being skinny. You want lean, trust me. Lean people are generally healthier and look better than skinny people.

When you close your eyes and picture yourself with your dream body, I can almost guarantee you you're picturing yourself more "lean" than "skinny". Not to mention there is a big chance the dream body in your head is 15-20 lbs. of muscle heavier than you are right now.

Instead of tracking the number on the scale, try getting used to tracking your body fat percentage. There are multiple options out there, including electronic handheld devices and Bluetooth smart scales, but I prefer the old-school skinfold caliper measurements and a flexible measuring tape. Do your own research and find what works best for you, or just go off the mirror results and compare some before and after pictures.

Speaking of pictures, you should take some once a week. Drop down to your underwear, or nothing at all, stand in front of a large mirror, hold up a piece of paper with your starting weight and date, and then take some photos of yourself from all angles. Lock them away on your phone, these are for your eyes only and just for self-tracking progress. A month down the road you won't remember what you looked like when you started, so having these will help you stay motivated and organized.

Whatever method you decide to go with for your tracking, consistency is key! Check yourself at the same time every single time. This is very important. There are so many factors that could skew your results like activity level, hydration level, humidity, and more. So for the most accurate tracking, do it as soon as you wake up before you eat or drink anything. This is also when to take your photos. Same time, same day, once a week, preferably at the end of the week and before any silly diet cheating or drinking.

Don't forget to write everything down somewhere and track the progress of your weight-lifting diet journey! Have no fear, I've got you covered there too. The back of this book has months of tracking charts for you to use.

It's important not to be tempted to weigh or track yourself every day. This is a fast track to getting discouraged. You can fluctuate in water weight alone by more than two pounds just because of a small diet change. You're just asking to be disappointed at that point.

What About Strength?

Oh strength, my sweet friend. Strength has been both separating and equalizing humans for centuries. Some people desire chiseled claves and 6% body fat, while others just want to squat 600 lbs.

About twice a year when I review my own training program in attempts to reignite my longing to be a USDA prime beef specimen, I wrestle with the internal struggle of deciding whether I want to be sculpted from marble or obtain vessel popping strength. A happy medium is normally where I settle, and where I have designed this program to lead you. It is a healthier, more realistic, and achievable physique.

Grown Man Strength

Having large muscles won't mean you're really strong, and being really strong won't mean you'll have large muscles. Some people are just born with the gift of strength or develop it over years of hard manual labor.

For example, my brother has never lifted weights a day in his life, yet I've seen him bench press a transmission into place underneath an F-350 and install it with the other hand by himself. It's often called country strong, farm strong, or grown man strength. It can be hidden under many layers of body fat, and you would never know it's there. So what gives?

Those country folks have technically been strength training their entire lives. Through means of manual labor like farming, working on cars, constructing a building, or pretty much anything else blue-collar, they've developed a low rep, high weight, lifting program without even knowing it. Top it all off with consistently working sun up to sun down 6 days a week, and a classic high caloric American diet, and you've got one homegrown strong man.

Multiple genetic and environmental factors come into play here. It could be anything from the length of their muscle fibers, to where those muscles attach to their bones. Some people are truly built differently.

Though lifting transmissions into undercarriages is not an easy feat, with any luck it will only have to be attempted once or twice before the job is done, so it's not nearly enough reps to tear the muscle in the way it needs to be torn to trigger hypertrophy. What it's really doing is *conditioning* the muscle rather than building the muscle.

The Happy Medium

Don't be sad little feller, you can have both. You can have an above-average amount of both muscle and strength.

The style of training I'm introducing you to, a PMO program, is designed to give you the best of both worlds when it comes to muscles and strength. The real difference that will set this program apart from most others will be your rep range, working weight, and lifting style.

I'll explain everything as we go, but here is a summary. 6-8 reps, for 3 sets, resting 2-3 minutes between sets, using mostly heavy compound lifts. Compound lifts are lifts that activate more than one muscle group at a time. Commonly referred to as old-school or Olympic lifts like squats, bench, deadlifts, etc.

Rep Range

This is a moderate rep range training program that uses the sweet spot of 6-8 reps. Women's rep range is a little different, but luckily I have a similar program book written for women Muscles Aren't Scary (see my social pages).

Outside of warm-ups, this will be your average rep range. Every workout every muscle group every time unless otherwise specified. Muscle groups like abs, triceps, and calves will have a high rep range due to their stubborn rebellious nature.

Your warm-up will be 1 set of 50% of your working weight for 10 reps, rest 1 minute, 1 more set of 50% for 10, rest 1 minute, 1 set of 75% for 5 reps, rest 1-2 minutes, 1 set of 90-95% for 2 reps, reset 3 minutes, first working set (see graph).

That would look something like this:

Warm-up Set 1	50 lbs.	10 reps
Rest 1 minute		
Warm-up Set 2	50 lbs.	10 reps
Rest 1 minute		
Warm-up Set 3	75 lbs.	5 reps
Rest 1-2 minutes		
Warm-up Set 4	90-95 lbs.	2 reps
Rest 3 minutes		

Note, your warm-up will only come before your first exercise station. For example, if your workout is a strict regimen of jump rope, hopscotch, pie eating, and finished with summersaults, you would only warm up before jump rope. Too much Warm-up can diminish lifting capacity, and glycogen storage (energy), thus reducing the desired amount of hypertrophy.

While we're on the topic of reps, let's talk about speed. It never fails, there will always be that one guy in the gym pushing out as many reps as fast as he can. You could be halfway across the gym and still feel the breeze off of his arm curls. This is a huge waste of time and energy... and also just looks ridiculous. He probably orders hot chocolate when he's at a coffee shop.

A proper rep has the muscle contracted and under stress the entire time. To do this our reps need to be slow and controlled in both directions, up and down. It is also important to ensure your form stays intact and that the correct muscles are being engaged. Going too fast will cause your form to diminish and reduce the tension your muscle is under on its way down.

Working Weight

As described earlier in the book, working weight is the standard weight you use during a specific exercise. How do you determine your working weight? No idea. Everyone is far too different for me to give you a formula to help you figure it out.

Just put some weight on the bar, about 75% of what you THINK you can do, and feel it out. We know our rep range is 6-8, so that means your working weight should be light enough to get at least 6 reps, but heavy enough to not get past 8 reps. Reps number 7 and 8 should be kicking your butt, if it's not, slowly add a little weight to the bar until it does.

I Found My Working Weight, Now What?

That will be your working weight for that one exercise until you're ready to increase it. When you can lift that weight for 3 sets of 8 reps without missing one, you can safely move up in weight next week. Remember each exercise will need its own working weight, it's not a universal number.

Increasing Weight

If the exercise is on a barbell, add 5 lbs. to each side of the bar (10 lbs. total) for your increase. If the exercise is on dumbbells, just go up 5 lbs. on each dumbbell for your increase.

That is now your new working weight and will be until you can lift it for 3 sets of 8 reps. Wash, rinse, and repeat.

Decreasing Weight

You don't. Unless injured/therapy. Listen to your doctor.

Stretching

You don't do that either, at least not before weightlifting. You should be warming up before, and stretching after. I know that may sound sacrilegious, but hear me out. A short bending or flexing motion to get the blood flowing is okay, but any stretching routine lasting more than 60 seconds has been shown to have diminishing effects on weightlifting. [5]

The type of stretching I'm telling you not to do (before a workout) is the longer duration *static stretching*. Static stretching is when you lengthen a muscle through means of pushing or pulling, and then holding it in that possession for a period of time. It's the classic stretching you were taught in middle school and carried with you as the standard for the rest of your life.

Holding a stretch like this diminishes your lifting capacity by removing some of the elasticity from the muscle. You want your muscles to be springy or more elastic...y when performing a lift, as lifting is just a muscle contracting and releasing over and over again.

Think about it like not wanting to overstretch a rubber band before using it, otherwise, it won't hold your item as tight as you need it to.

What we want is a good warm-up like the one I detailed for you earlier. Warming up is technically a type of *dynamic or active stretching*. Stretching that involves muscle movement within its natural range of motion for shorter periods of time. A good comparison of the two would be doing a couple of air squats before hitting the squat rack vs. a full-length hamstring/quad stretch-and-hold.

Rest

Resting between sets is important. Since the way I've designed this program is to constantly overload the muscle, you'll need a minimum of 2-3 minutes of rest between each set. This may be longer than some other programs you will hear about, but a PMO program is different and will require this. It assures the muscle is rested, primed and ready to lift something heavy for 2 more sets.

Off Day Rest

Depending on whether you pick the 3-day plan or the 5-day plan, you will have anywhere from 4-2 rest and recovery days where you're not going to the gym.

It is still advised that 1 or 2 of those days you get in some form of activity like a light walk, bike ride, intense game of table tennis, or anything of that nature. This is referred to as active recovery.

Active recovery is good as it increases the heart rate just a little and allows the blood to better flow through the muscles providing them with more of the nutrients they require. Recover will be covered in more detail in its own chapter.

3 NUTRITION BRIEFING

Have you ever heard the expression that getting a good-looking body is just 20% in the gym and 80% diet? Though I understand the message here, I disagree with that way of thinking completely. You workout in a gym, and you eat in a kitchen, two different places at two different times, so why are we dividing percentages here? Your mindset should be 100% gym, and 100% diet.

This chapter is going to cover the basics of nutrition and its role in body composition, alcohol calorie tracking, and diet cheating.

I know I've already beaten to death the fact that you need to be feeding your muscles, but I haven't really told you how you should be feeding them. Later on in the chapter *Diet Assigned,* when I finally give you your diet, you will have 3 options to choose from, cutting (burning fat), bulking (gaining muscle), or maintaining (a very long and very slow burning of fat and gaining of muscle). All 3 of those diets vary in calories and macronutrient breakdowns, but the basic nutritional guidelines you learn here in this chapter still apply to all 3. This is called *counting your macros.*

Quality and Quantity

Quality

The big question is, does quality matter? Well, we already know a calorie is just a unit used to measure energy, and the only way to lose weight is to be in a calorie deficit so your body can burn the energy it has in storage. So if we are strictly talking about our body's law of thermodynamics (energy in vs. energy out) then no, quality doesn't matter.

Where things start to get a little tricky is body composition and trying to keep up with supply and demand inside of your body. You can technically lose weight by eating brownies, but our bodies need far more nutrients than what you'll find there. For starters, they're very low in protein, so your muscle mass will suffer greatly if all you eat is brownies, duh.

But what if we added protein shakes? So we'd just be eating brownies and drinking enough protein shakes to maintain our muscles. So long as you were in a slight calorie deficit (or surpluses) at the end of the day, and getting enough protein shakes in, this would work without a doubt. How do we know this? A calorie is a calorie, energy is energy, and a deficit is a deficit, it's basic science. You wouldn't be rich in micronutrients, but you could still get sauced.

Maybe a better question would be one of sustainability. How long could we eat like before risking our health? We have to separate counting calories from being healthy. They are not the same. Yes, we can get sexy off of brownies and protein, but we also must acknowledge there is very little nutrition there. Just because you're on a diet and counting your calories, doesn't make you a healthy person. This is my main gripe with average calorie-counting people on Keto diets. I find it hard to convince myself that filling a bell pepper with mayonnaise, sour cream, bacon, and cheese is healthy diet food. That person may be in a calorie deficit and losing weight, but that person is not healthy. We know better than that. So in this case, yes, quality matters. Balance matters.

You will have to find the balance for yourself as you journey through watching what you eat now. I try to follow a 90/10 rule no matter what my fitness goals are. For each day I eat 90% clean like a good boy and eat 10% like I'm on the naughty list and just don't care. No additional calories, just a little 10% splurge, normally to shut my sweet tooth up.

Quantity

Quantity is a no-brainer for a guy like me, but you may be different. I would rather eat foods that are lower in calories but higher in volume because I just like to eat. As an example, take a bowl of chicken and rice and throw a few handfuls of lettuce or cabbage in there. That adds less than 20 calories, but 2 cups of volume. Some people are happy with just the chicken and rice, but that's not me.

Quantity also begs the question, how many meals per day and when? Some people say 6 meals a day is the magic number, and others say 3, so which is it? It doesn't freaking matter. Remember the thermodynamics we talked about, and how long food is digested in our bodies?

This will just be up to your personal preference. No matter what anyone tells you, there are no wrong answers here. Say it with me people, calories in vs. calories out. Don't overcomplicate things.

Eating Pre and Post Training

Yes to both. Your hippie gym friends will probably say something like having a protein shake right after a workout is good because your body is in an anabolic window that only lasts 30 minutes. While that's not terrible advice, it's also not completely true.

Your body is in fact in a prime anabolic state right after a workout, but it can last upwards of two hours in some people. You should definitely eat something as soon as you can just to go ahead and get those calories in to aid in the muscle recovery, but if you have to wait an hour or so, it's no big deal[6]. Your body will still use and appreciate the meal whenever you eat it.

I will break down exactly how much of what to eat before and after a little later on.

Hydration

Let's just keep this one short and simple. Water is good, drink water.

Drink at least 1 gallon of water, every single day no excuses. If you're crazy about tracking your BMI and body composition, this is especially important to pay attention to. Drink the same amount of water every day so that your tracking won't be skewed by water weight and fluctuation. Never drink less, and try not to drink more unless you need it. 1 gallon is plenty for almost everyone. Maybe a little more on sauna or heavy cardio days if you decide to do those.

Alcohol

A strange beast to deal with. The easiest thing for me to tell you is to avoid it. It really offers no value to you and you don't need it, but I'm also not a deranged idiot. People drink, so let's talk about how to do it and how to keep track of it.

The Dilemma

Alcohol calories are strange. We already talked about the nutrients we eat that actually contain calories, protein with 4 calories per gram, carbs with 4 calories per gram, and fat with 9 calories per gram. Now let's compare that to some of the bestselling low calories beers in America.

The slim canned 95 calorie lite beer with a proclaimed 2.6 carbs per 12 oz. It shall remain unnamed, but let's math. 2.6 (carbs per can) multiplied by 4 (calories per carb) equals 10.4 calories from carbs per can. There is no protein and no fat in this beverage... so where are the other 84.6 calories coming from?

The brown whiskey from Kentucky born in charred oak barrels. 97 calories in 1 shot, no carbs, no protein, and no fat, so what gives?

Long story short, alcohol is just built differently. It's not even required to be on nutrition labels in the United States[17], it's classified as *optional*.

There are actually 7 calories per gram of alcohol but it is not a necessary substance for humans, so isn't counted as a nutrient. Our bodies treat alcohol as a toxin and the only way to get rid of that toxin is to metabolize it in the liver and use it as energy or pee it out[18]. The only problem is we're not sure how much we're burning vs. peeing. It's different for all races, genders, and builds of people.

In the fitness world, the solution everyone seems to agree on here is counting all calories in the beverage as if they were all carbs or all fat. For example, if the beer has 95 calories, that's really like having 24 carbs or 10.55 grams of fat taken from your allotted amounts. Now you can see how these beverages can add up.

Diet Cheating

I want you to cheat on your diet. It can be good for replenishing your glycogen stores and mental sanity. However, it can also ruin an entire week's worth of work if you just eat everything in sight for an entire day. Let me teach you how to do it right, so you can splurge on the goods while still looking like the Prince of Masculinity.

We don't do cheat days here, so just go ahead and erase that phrase from your memory. We do cheat *meals*, just 1 per week because we're a civilized people. Eat whatever you want for your cheat meal, even desert, but it must all be in one sitting. You can't just decide to come back for dessert 2 hours later.

If you want to increase your results and maximize the potential of your "cheating", consider doing a refeed day instead. A refeed day is an entire day of eating outside of your regular diet. You increase your eating by 500 calories in just carbohydrates (125g), keep your protein the same, and fats as low as possible. This also only comes once a week and is designed to fully replenish your glycogen storage.

If you are bulking there is no reason to refeed, so just stick to the cheat meal. If you are on maintenance you can pick between the two (refeed would be better) and if you are cutting I highly recommend refeeding as it will be far more beneficial, but if you want a cheat meal instead, go for it.

Your diet should be the same before and after your cheat meal, we're not trying to fit this into our macros, this is to be extra food and extra calories. Consider doing this the day before a large muscle group like legs or back. You will have plenty of nutrients stored to rock those lifts even harder.

Don't freak out if you look a little different in the mirror the next morning. Sometimes cheat meals and refeeds will make you look pumped and sexy, but other times a little bloated and puffy. This is normal and to be expected.

Do not skip cheat meals or reefed days. Some people can get away with only doing it once every two weeks, but I wouldn't go any longer than that. Your progress can potentially halt without it. Your muscles need it.

The Truth

Modern diets suck. The majority of our foods, even our health foods, have been processed beyond recognition or so massively overproduced that they lack the nutrients they once had. That has led to over 1/3 of the world's population being deficient in iron, iodine, calcium, magnesium, and vitamins A, B12, and D3. [7]

Modern Lifestyles also suck. We spend way too much time inside working and watching TV, instead of being active outside. Did you know your body produces vitamins when exposed to moderate amounts of sunlight?

The truth is it's very hard to get everything your body needs nowadays without supplementation. That's just the world we live in. Thankfully we cover supplements with an entire chapter later on in this book.

4 CARDIO

Cardio is my sworn enemy. I can't stand it. Unfortunately, it's necessary, and it's good for you. In this chapter we will cover why cardio is needed, how much is needed, and when to do it in relation to your training.

Why Is Cardio Needed

First things first, cardio burns calories and can help burn body fat. You might argue so does working out, and so does dieting in a deficit. Yes, all of those things will burn calories and help us burn body fat, but cardio sure can help.

Cardio is there to be an assisting component along our fat-burning adventure so we don't have to do crazy amounts of those other things. For example, if you want to burn three thousand calories a week, you are going to divide and conquer. Burn a little by cardio, burn a little by working out, and burn a little by eating less. You could just remove the calories from your weekly diet, but doesn't eating more food and just doing just a little extra cardio sound better than removing 3,000 calories of precious snacks?

Not to mention cardio has been shown to lower cholesterol, lower blood pressure, regulate blood sugar, strengthen your immune system, improve your sleep, improved joint mobility, better distribute nutrition and oxygen, improve mood health, improve brain function, and so much more. [8]

How Much Cardio Is Needed

Now would be a good time for me to quote my medical disclaimer found at the front of this book, talk to your freaking doctor. Everyone has different limits. Understanding your limits, or at least knowing when you've reached them is important. Safety first.

The amount of cardio needed depends on the number of calories you desire to burn and/or not burn. There is a bare minimum I suggest you do regardless of your goals just to take care of your heart, mind, and body. Below is a chart to help visualize a schedule. Below the chart, you will find detailed descriptions and explanations.

The Bare Minimum

HITT	10 minutes	X2 weekly
Jogging	30 minutes	X2 weekly
Bike Ride	45 minutes	X2 weekly
Long Walk/Hike	1 hour	X2 weekly

You will find that the cardio listed above will increase in time as it decreases in intensity. The less time you have, the more intense the cardio will need to be.

HITT High-Intensity Interval Training

This type of cardio has been crowned king when it comes to

effective calorie and fat burning. Designed to be a system of high intensity, low intensity, high intensity, over and over again for predetermined timed intervals.

For example, sprinting as hard as you can for 1 minute, then walking for 1 minute, repeated over and over again for 10 minutes.

This is great because it can be super universal. Are you extremely out of shape? No problem, just change your interval times to something like sprinting for 10 seconds, and walking for 30. Gradually increase the intensity until you're a certified stud machine.

Are you someone who has problems with impacting joints while running? No problem, this can be done on a bike, elliptical, treadmill, or even a pool. It's super universal and only takes 10 minutes.

Steady Jogging

This may be self-explanatory but I'll cover it just in case it's needed. Jogging is cardio that is lower intensity than running, but higher intensity than walking. Your heart rate should be moderately elevated the entire time and you shouldn't be stopping.

If you're going to jog for only 30 minutes, you need to find the speed your body can handle for that entire 30 minutes. This may be pretty slow for some people, but that's okay. The idea is to gradually increase speed over time.

Jogging on earthy terrain is better for your joints than jogging on asphalt or pavement. The softer ground and changes in elevation make for a good workout. Tracks at high schools and colleges are also nice and easy on the joints, but jogging in a repetitive circle is for... squares.

Bike Ride

Bike riding is my preferred form of cardio. Not only is it low impact on the joints, but it also promotes muscle building. A bike ride with terrain and elevation changes can be a good workout for the legs as pushing down on the pedals closely mimics the same movements made when performing a squat.

Walking/Hiking

This is known as *steady-state cardio*. It may take longer than all of the other forms of cardio I have listed, but it's also much less intense and easier on the body.

The walk needs to be more than just a walk in the park. Hills inclines, and terrain changes would make it better and just a little more challenging. Even a walk on the beach would be preferred over a walk in the park as walking in the sand will use more muscles than a walk on the pavement.

Steady-state cardio can even be done for pleasure. Didn't have time to do cardio during the week? Play a trick on your loved ones by telling them you're going on a hike Saturday morning. It may seem like a fun weekend activity for the family, but it's really just your low-key plan to get totally ripped. You can even take the dog.

When To Do Cardio

If you're squeezing in cardio on your off days, then *when* doesn't matter. A lot of silly gooses will tell you that fasted cardio (cardio on an empty stomach) is better for burning fat because you're using fuel already stored in your body, but we've already established that the only way to burn fat is to be in a calorie deficit, and everything else is malarkey and needs more data[10]. Just do your cardio when you feel like doing your cardio because you're a free man.

If you're doing your cardio on the same days you're lifting weights, you should be paying a little more attention as to when you're doing it. The options are before, or after.

The short answer is after. To put it as simply as I can, why would you use up all of the energy you have stored in your muscle for cardio? That energy should be used for lifting your hardest and heaviest, producing more hypertrophy, and promoting more growth.

Ideally, cardio should be done 2-4 hours after weightlifting so the muscle is sure to replenish the energy you just used, but who the heck has time for that? If you don't, just squeeze it in after your workout and before your post-gym snacks.

Too Much Cardio

Yes, you can do too much cardio[9], especially if you're not eating enough. Not eating enough and doing cardio is worst for you than not eating enough and sitting on the couch. Go do an internet search and compare marathon runners and then track stars. One of them will have far more muscle mass than the other. The quick explanation is one burns too many calories doesn't recover long enough or their bodies just can consume enough calories to keep up.

When you do cardio, you are using multiple muscles and causing micro-tears in all of them. Your body wants to heal that muscle, it's a natural automatic response. To do that it needs nutrients (food). If you continue to use that muscle and neglect to feed it enough, your muscle will start to break down, soften, and shrink, this is referred to as a catabolic response. It's a survival response from your body. Having more muscle requires more work for your body and in order for your body to do that work, it must be fed. Otherwise, your body says "I don't have enough nutrients to maintain this large amount of sexy muscle, I better get rid of it so I have enough nutrients to spread around".

5 RECOVERY

We've already covered some basic recovery stuff, but having a little deeper understanding will help you along your muscle-building adventure.

Proper recovery requires rest, nutrition, and some mild therapeutic activities. I know the last part sounds a little complicated, but it just means massaging and stretching.

Stretching

Stretching should ideally be done right after a workout. Whatever muscle group you just finished working out should be the one you're stretching. I understand it may sound a little aggravating to divide your gym time between lifting, cardio, and now stretching. You're probably thinking you'll go well over the 45-60 minute time block I promised. If you try to squeeze all that in, then yes, you will go over. That's why I recommend you do active recovery on your off days, as opposed to just lazy lounging couch days.

Saving the cardio and stretching for your off days can help you beat the gym clock on your workout days. Note: If you're only going to be stretching one day a week, it needs to be a solid 30-45 minutes of whole-body stretching. You can couple this time with watching TV, reading a book, or getting it in just before bed.

At the end of this chapter, you will find a whole-body stretching routine with images to assist you along the way. If you're going to try and stretch at the end of each workout, just pick a few stretches for that muscle group you can spend at least 5 minutes on.

Massage'ish type things
Not many people can afford a full-body deep tissue massage once a week, but that doesn't mean we can't find a few easy cheap ways to get those same benefits.

Catching These Hands
You can try massaging yourself. Some body parts are pretty easy to get to with your own hands. If your hands aren't enough for you, try a vibrating massage gun. They're worth every penny. I bought specially made attachments that turned my jigsaw into a massage gun.

Balls
Applying pressure to the problem area with a tennis or lacrosse ball can help focus all of the force directly where you want it. If your back, butt, or hips are hurting, try lying on top of it with the ball under the problem area. The pressure alone could be enough to alleviate pain in some people, but others may need to roll and gyrate while lying on the ball to really get the fuss worked out.

Foam Rolling

Came out in the 1970s but I don't recall it being mainstream and widely adopted until the early 2000s. Now it's in everyone's hearts forever. It really is that good.

If you've ever been to a gym and seen someone rolling around on a long tube of foam moaning, laughing, and crying at the same time, that was foam rolling

Despite what you may think, it's actually not a form of interpretive dance, it's used to relieve muscle pain. This is done by rolling the problem area over the roller and only applying the pressure of your body weight. The foam roller will always maintain contact with the ground, you just slide your body parts back and forth over it. They come in many shapes and sizes, but the application remains the same. Just roll and moan.

Sauna

The hot, steamy, incredibly humid, terribly uncomfortable environment that people pay money to sit in. Traditional sauna conditions are created with hot stones, water, and steam reaching upwards of 200 °F, but now that we live in the future, inferred lights are used to create a similar experience at only 100-150 °F. As long as your doctor is okay with it, the sauna is an awesome recovery tool, and also comes with the benefits I have listed below. [11]

Improved Blood Flow

The heat relaxes and dilates blood vessels, making it easier for your body to pump. This improved blood flow naturally increases the amount of nutrients flowing to your muscles, and brain[12].

Improved Mood Health/Stress Relief

By releasing beta-endorphins and spreading them throughout the body producing a feeling of euphoria. Many workouts can also do this, but it is particularly evident with sauna usage. [12]

Pain Relieving Properties

By releasing multiple anti-inflammatory hormones like adrenaline, noradrenaline, and IGF-1 (insulin growth factor) [12]

Heat Shock Protein Production

This is a bit much but stay with me. The protein molecules in our bodies are constructed and behave in a specific manner, but when they are damaged their half-life gets disrupted and they don't leave the body like they're supposed to. This causes broken proteins to stay in the body too long and become aggregated with other broken proteins (protein aggregation).

Protein aggregation plays a large role in brain aging, Alzheimer's, Parkinson's, and cardiovascular diseases.

Heat Shock Proteins repair these broken proteins and lowers the body's accumulation of aggregated proteins, reducing the risk of the mentioned diseases by upwards of 40%. [13]

This goes way too deep for me to try and explain the rest, but you can check out anything from Dr. Rhonda Patrick about heat shock proteins for more information.

Icing and Heating

While we're on the subject of hot environments, let's talk about applying heat or icing an injury. [14] [15]

Does it matter which one I use?

Kinda. Heating and icing are used for different types of soreness and injuries, however, you can have an injury that is a little more complex and may require both.

Heat - Being a vasodilator, increases blood flow and will give the area a feeling of being loose as it relaxes the muscles and blood vessels. [14] [15]

Cold – A vasoconstrictor, doing the opposite by constricting the blood vessels and fluid flow, working as a natural anti-inflammatory. [14] [15]

So for example, getting out of bed and being stiff from sleeping wrong, you would use heat. An old injury from your glory days sneaking back up, use heat for that too. A newer sore joint from too much yard work or weight lifting, ice that. Shin splints from cardio impact, ice it.

The golden rule of temperature injury application here is 20 minutes on 20 minutes off. Don't be afraid to try both even if you don't fall under one of the examples I listed. Some people just respond differently.

Sleep

That thing you always hear growing up, "8 hours of sleep is what you need", is the real deal. If you're not sleeping, you're not recovering enough to keep up with what you're putting your body through. 6 hours is the bare minimum. Anything below that can be detrimental for things like blood pressure, diabetes, heart attack, heart failure, stroke, obesity, depression, reduced immune system function, and lower sex drive. [19] [20]

If you're not sleeping well, you may consider some form

of supplementation. I would start with natural remedies, over the counter aids, and then if it's still not working, speak to your doctor about other options. Sleep is probably the most important thing on this list, do not underestimate it.

THE STRETCHING ROUTINE I PROMISED

The next few pages are pictures and descriptions of stretches. There is a darkened portion of each photo that will indicate the muscle/area it's designed to stretch. Hold each stretch for the 3 sets of 10 seconds per limb.

You'll notice a lot of them will focus on the back and leg areas, and that's by design. Remember that everything is connected, and stretching those large muscle groups will lead to an all-around more comfortable muscle structure.

Hamstring and back – Standing with your legs a shoulders width apart, knees just slightly bent, bend over at your hips, and aim to touch your toes. Your legs shouldn't be bending any further from where you started. Push down with your shoulders to activate the back stretching. Feel it in your back, hamstrings, and calves.

Bent Over Core Stretch – Standing with feet together, tighten your core and bend over at the waist. Allow your arms to hand and keep the core tight. Feel it in your core and down your spine

Lumbar Extension – Standing with your feet together and back straight, bend backwards and hang your arms behind your legs. Take this one slow so you're sure not to fall. Feel it down your back and spine.

Side Oblique Stretch – Standing straight, and with your hands laced together above your head. Tighten your core and lean to the side and hold. Feel it in your obliques.

Hanging Back Stretch – This one is pretty simple. While hanging from a bar, relax your back and shoulder muscles. Feel a pull across your entire back and down your spine.

Cross Arm Back and Shoulder – Standing up straight, fold one arm across your chest, then fold your other arm up over it pulling it in towards your chest. Feeling the stretch across the shoulder, and back area.

Neck Stretch – Standing or seated, place both hands on the back of your neck, then pull it down and in towards your chest while tucking your chin. You can rotate this stretch in all directions your neck will do. Keep your back straight. Feel it in the neck.

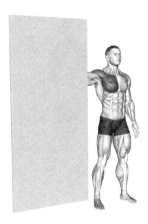

Chest Door Stretch – Find a wall or door jamb and place one arm on the backside of it, then lean forward and rotate with your torso. Feel it in your chest and upper shoulder.

World's Best Stretch – Yes that is the actual name. Start by assuming a pushup position. Bring one leg up where the foot is parallel with your shoulder. Bring up your arm (same side as the leg you chose) and extend it towards the sky while routing your torso outwards. Feel it across your legs, back, and core.

Calves Stretch – Sitting on your butt, tuck one leg into your crotch area, fully extend the other one, reach forward with both hands and bend your foot towards your chest. Feel it in your calves.

Frog Stretch – Sitting on your butt, tuck both feet in towards your crotch area and push your knees as close to the ground as you can. Feel it in your hamstrings and inner thigh (the adductors muscle group).

Adductor Muscle Stretch – Lying flat on your back, legs together and up at a straight 90°, slowly spread your legs, like an eagle if you will, and feel the pull in the muscles of your inner thigh area.

Single Leg Pull – Lying on your back with legs fully extended out in front of you, bend one leg at the knee and pull it in towards your chest. Feel it in your hamstrings.

T Spine Mobility Stretch – Lying flat on your back with legs in front of you, arms out wide (body in the shape of a T), pick one leg up, bend it at the knee, and while rotating at the hip, bring that leg to the opposite side as close to the ground as you can. Feel it in your glutes, lower back, and obliques.

Quad Stretch – Standing up with your legs together, bring one leg up behind you and grab it with your hand. Pull that foot up and in towards your back. Feel it in your quads.

End of stretching routine

Do the whole thing or pick a few per day, just make sure you get some sort of stretching in during the week. Stretching will keep your body mobile and primed for lifting and recovery.

6 PROGRAM ASSIGNED

Now is when you decide whether you're going to do the 3-day or the 5-day program. 5 being better than 3 of course, but 3 being more than adequate for our time-sensitive friends.

Each program will have your days broken down into muscle groups. You can choose which days you want to be your rest days. I personally go Monday-Friday weightlifting and rest Saturday-Sunday with some form of stretching and cardio tossed in. If you're going to do the 3-day program, consider not taking your 4 days of rest all in a row. Something close to every other day works best.

The 3-day program is going to be jammed packed so we can get everything done we need in so few days. Don't get distracted in the gym by talking to everyone and making nice, this will slow you down and you'll miss your time mark.

Keep in mind that your first couple of workouts may last longer than the 45-60 minutes I promised until you figure out the lay of the land. Once you hammer all of it out, you'll be flying through there in no time. Now, let's take a look at the programs. At the end of this chapter I will have detailed descriptions and pictures of each workout, so don't worry if something seems unfamiliar to you at first. Don't forget about the free tracking sheets in the back of this book for when you start this program.

3 DAY PROGRAM

Day 1	*Chest, shoulders, triceps*
Day 2	*Back, biceps, abs*
Day 3	*Legs*

Day 1	
Exercise 1	**Incline Bench Press Barbell**
	Warm-ups followed by 3 working sets 6-8 reps
Exercise 2	**Flat Bench Press Barbell**
	3 working sets 6-8 reps
Exercise 3	**Flat Bench Chest Fly**
	3 working sets 6-8 reps
Exercise 4	**Overhead Press Standing or Seated**
	3 working sets 6-8 reps
Exercise 5	**Dumbbell Lateral Raise**
	3 working sets 6-8 reps
Exercise 6 Super Set	**Tri Extensions – Diamond Pushups**
	3 Super Sets (10-15 reps each)
Day 2	
Exercise 1	**Deadlift**
	Warm-ups followed by 3 working sets 6-8 reps
Exercise 2	**Bent Over Rows**
	3 working sets 6-8 reps
Exercise 3	**Pull-ups (weighted when possible)**
	3 working sets 6-8 reps
Exercise 4	**Alternating Dumbbell Curls**
	3 working sets 6-8 reps
Exercise 5 Super Set	**Hanging Leg Raises – Crunches**
	3 Super Sets (10-15 reps each)

Day 3	
Exercise 1	**Squats** *Warm-ups followed by 3 working sets 6-8 reps*
Exercise 2	**Leg Press or Front Squats** *3 working sets 6-8 reps*
Exercise 3	**Romanian Deadlifts** *3 working sets 6-8 reps*
Exercise 4 Super Set	**Weighted Calf Raises – Unweighted** *3 Super Sets (10-15 reps each)*

5 DAY PROGRAM

Day 1	*Chest, Triceps*
Day 2	*Back, Biceps*
Day 3	*Shoulders, Abs*
Day 4	*Legs*
Day 5	*Arms, abs*

Day 1	
Exercise 1	**Incline Bench Press Barbell** *Warm-ups followed by 3 working sets 6-8 reps*
Exercise 2	**Flat Bench Press Dumbbell** *3 working sets 6-8 reps*
Exercise 3	**Incline Bench Chest Fly** *3 working sets 6-8 reps*
Exercise 4	**Close Grip Bench Press** *3 working sets 6-8 reps*
Exercise 5	**Tri Extensions** *3 working sets 10-15 reps*

Day 2	
Exercise 1	**Deadlifts** *Warm-ups followed by 3 working sets 6-8 reps*
Exercise 2	**Bent Over Rows** *3 working sets 6-8 reps*
Exercise 3	**Pull-Ups (weighted if possible)** *3 working sets 6-8 reps*
Exercise 4	**Rear Delt Raise** *3 working sets 6-8 reps*
Exercise 5	**Alternating Dumbbell Curls** *3 working sets 6-8 reps*

Day 3	
Exercise 1	**Overhead Press Barbell** *Warm-ups followed by 3 working sets 6-8 reps*
Exercise 2	**Overhead Press Dumbbell** *3 working sets 6-8 reps*
Exercise 3	**Shrugs** *3 working sets 6-8 reps*
Exercise 4	**Dumbbell Lateral Raise** *3 working sets 6-8 reps*
Exercise 5	**Crunches** *3 working sets 10-15 reps*
Exercise 6 Super Set	**Hanging Leg Raises** *3 working sets 10-15 reps*

Day 4	
Exercise 1	**Squats** *Warm-ups followed by 3 working sets 6-8 reps*
Exercise 2	**Leg Press or Front Squats** *3 working sets 6-8 reps*
Exercise 3	**Romanian Deadlifts** *3 working sets 6-8 reps*
Exercise 4	**Barbell Plate Calf Raises** *3 working sets 10-15 reps*
Exercise 5	**Unweighted Calf Raises** *3 working sets 10-15 reps*

Day 5	
Exercise 1	**Alternated Dumbbell Curls** *Warm-ups followed by 3 working sets 6-8 reps*
Exercise 2	**Alternating Hammer Curls** *3 working sets 6-8 reps*
Exercise 3	**Tri Extensions** *3 working sets 10-15 reps*
Exercise 4	**Diamond Pushups** *3 working sets 10-15 reps*
Exercise 5	**Crunches** *3 working sets 10-15 reps*
Exercise 6	**Hanging Leg Raises** *3 working sets 10-15 reps*

Do your program for 10 weeks, and then I want you to take a whole week off. Use that week to spend time with family, catch up with friends, and physically recover. Your diet (assigned next chapter) will not change. This is not a cheat week to eat like a truck driver, and you will still need to do your cardio. Some form of active recovery and stretching is still recommended on the days you'd normally be training.

The next few pages will be pictures and instructions for the lifts I have assigned you. If there is something you don't understand or I didn't explain well enough, just internet search for a video explanation for further assistance.

FLAT BENCH PRESS (BARBELL)

On a flat level bench, lay back and place your hands on the bar, they should be slightly wider than shoulder-width apart, and with knuckles towards the ceiling. Lift the bar out of the rack and press it up until your arms are extended and your hands are above your pectoral muscles. Slowly lower the bar down to your chest, then press it back up again. Repeat processes until exhaustion or reps are met.

FLAT BENCH PRESS (DUMBBELL)

On a flat level bench, lay back and bring the dumbbells to the loaded position as seen in the left photo, they should be slightly wider than shoulder-width apart, and with knuckles towards the ceiling. Slowly lift the dumbbells pressing them up until your arms are extended and your hands are above your pectoral muscles. Slowly lower them back to loaded position and repeat processes until exhaustion or reps are met.

INCLINE BENCH PRESS (BARBELL)

Set bench to 30-45° angle. Sit back and place your hands on the bar, they should be slightly wider than shoulder-width apart, and with knuckles towards the ceiling. Lift the bar out of the rack and press it up until your arms are extended and your hands are above your shoulders. Slowly lower the bar to your chest, then press it back up again. Repeat processes until exhaustion or reps are met.

INCLINE BENCH PRESS (DUMBBELL)

Set bench to 30-45° angle. Sit back and bring the dumbbells to the loaded position as seen in the left photo. They should be slightly wider than shoulder-width apart, elbows slightly below parallel, and knuckles towards the ceiling. Slowly lift the dumbbells pressing them up until your arms are extended and your hands are above your shoulders. Slowly lower them back down to the loaded position and repeat processes until exhaustion or reps are met.

CLOSE GRIP BENCH PRESS (BARBELL)

On a flat level bench, lay back and place your hands on the bar, they should be in line with the center of your pectoral muscles, and with knuckles towards the ceiling. Lift the bar out of the rack and press it up until your arms are extended and your hands are above your pectoral muscles. Slowly lower the bar down to your chest, then press it back up again. Repeat processes until exhaustion or reps are met.

FLAT BENCH CHEST FLY (DUMBBELL)

On a flat level bench, lay back and bring the dumbbells to the loaded position as seen in the right photo. They should be extended up above your pectoral muscles with a slight bend in the elbow, and knuckles towards the ceiling. Slowly open your arms bringing the dumbbells out until your upper arms are parallel to the floor. Now slowly bring them back to the loaded position while keeping the bend in the elbow. It should look as if you are hugging a large tree. Repeat processes until exhaustion or reps are met.

INCLINE BENCH CHEST FLY (DUMBBELL)

Set bench to 30-45° angle. Sit back and bring the
dumbbells to the loaded position as seen in the right photo.
They should be extended up above your shoulder muscles
with a slight bend in the elbow, and knuckles towards the
ceiling. Slowly open your arms bringing the dumbbells out
until your upper arms are parallel to your chest line. Now
slowly bring them back to the loaded position while
keeping the bend in the elbow. It should look as if you are
hugging a large tree. Repeat processes until exhaustion or
reps are met

TRICEPS EXTENSION (DUMBBELL)

Standing or seated, grab a dumbbell with both hands and extend it above and behind your head. Slowly lower the dumbbell until your elbows are at a 45° angle, then push it back up to the loaded position. Try to keep your elbows pointed in as much as possible when performing this lift. Repeat processes until exhaustion or reps are met.

DIAMOND PUSHUPS

On level ground, assume the loaded pushup position shown on the left. Bring your hands in towards the center, and using the index finger and thumb of each hand make a diamond shape by bringing their tips together on the ground. This should be right below your pectoral muscles.

Slowly lower your body to the ground as low as you can, then push yourself back up to the loaded position. Keep your elbows and arms tucked in throughout the exercise. Repeat processes until exhaustion or reps are met.

If you cannot perform this style of pushup, try keeping your knees on the ground for the first few weeks. Commonly referred to as a "girl pushup" while we were in grade school. Don't be ashamed or embarrassed, we all have to start somewhere.

DEADLIFT (BARBELL)

Standing with your feet shoulder-width apart, squat down and grab the bar with your hands just outside your legs. Bring your butt down below your shoulders keeping your back straight (see image left). Lift the bar by driving your hips forward and legs up. Be very sure to keep your back straight, and the bar close to your legs during the entire lift. Lower the bar back down the way it came in a controlled manner. **Repeat processes until exhaustion or reps are met.**

BENT OVER ROWS (BARBELL)

Standing with your feet shoulder-width apart, bend over at the waist and hold the barbell with your hands just outside of your legs. Slightly bend your knees and look down aligning your neck and spine making sure to keep your back straight. Let the bar hang down with your arms straight.
Tighten your core and squeeze your delts and lats together while using your arms to pull (row) the weight up until it touches your stomach, then slowly lower it back down. The bar should stay close to your legs throughout the lift.
Repeat processes until exhaustion or reps are met.

REAR DELT RAISE

Seated or standing, legs together, hanging arms down with elbows slightly bent. Hold your dumbbells outside of your legs with palms facing each other and knuckles pointed to the ground. While maintaining a straight spine and neck, slowly lift your arms up and out until your upper arms are parallel to your delts. Repeat processes until exhaustion or reps are met.

PULL-UPS

Grab a bar. Pull yourself up. Don't be cheap with them, all the way down, all the way up.

Grip doesn't matter as much as you've been lead to believe, do what you want.

If you can't do a pull-up, try wrapping some workout bands around the bar and then around your foot to assist you.

ALTERNATING DUMBBELL CURLS

Standing or seated, hold the dumbbells down by your sides on the outside of your body. One at a time slowly bring the dumbbell up using your elbow as the pivot point, not your shoulder. The upper portion of your arm shouldn't move. Bring it all the way up until you've maxed your range of motion near your chin, then slowly lower it back down. The dumbbell should be held in a horizontal position throughout the lift. Alternate sides, counting individual reps for each arm. Repeat processes until exhaustion or reps are met.

ALTERNATING HAMMER CURLS

Standing or seated, hold the dumbbells down by your sides on the outside of your body. One at a time slowly bring the dumbbell up and inwards to your chest using your elbow as the pivot point, not your shoulder. The upper portion of your arm shouldn't move. Bring it all the way up until you've maxed your range of motion under your chin, then slowly lower it back down. The dumbbell should be held in the vertical position throughout the lift. Alternate sides, counting individual reps for each arm. Repeat processes until exhaustion or reps are met.

STANDING OVERHEAD PRESS (BARBELL)

Standing with your feet shoulder-width apart and barbell in the loaded position above your chest, shown in the left photo, slowly lift the bar above your head fully extending your arms while keeping your core tight. Now slowly lower the bar back down to the loaded position. Repeat processes until exhaustion or reps are met.

Some people debate whether the bar should be in front of your head or behind it. Do whatever feels best to you. I feel better shoulder isolation going behind the head.

This can also be done seated and/or with a dumbbell. The same basic principles will apply.

SIDE LATERAL RAISE

Standing with your feet together, waist and elbows slightly bent, hold the dumbbells in front of your body, resting just off of your quads. Slowly bring them up and out keeping the same bend in your elbows. Bring them up until the tops of your arms are parallel with your shoulders. Repeat processes until exhaustion or reps are met.

SHRUGS (BARBELL)

Standing with your feet shoulder-width apart, holding the bar with your hands just outside of your legs. Lift your shoulders straight up, hold for one second, then lower them back down. Repeat processes until exhaustion or reps are met.

Make sure you keep your shoulders back and your back straight.

SQUAT (BARBELL)

Standing under a loaded barbell with your feet shoulder-
width apart, toes slightly pointed outward, and core
tighten, slowly lower your body until your quads are
parallel to the floor at a minimum, but I suggest you go as
low as possible to maximize your range of motion here.
Slowly push with your legs and bring the weight back up.
Keep your chest up, back straight, and your eyes forward
thought the entire lift. Repeat processes until exhaustion or
reps are met.

The bar should rest on the line where your upper shoulders
meet your trapezius muscles.

LEG PRESS

The only machine you will see in this program. This workout can be substituted for front squats if your gym doesn't have one. Front squats will be explained next.

Lay down on the machine, bring your legs up to the center of the platform, and spread your feet shoulder-width apart. Use your legs to release the machine off of the rack and slowly lower the weight down. Your legs should meet a 90° angle at a minimum, but you should go deeper if possible. Now slowly push the weight back up. Repeat processes until exhaustion or reps are met.

FRONT SQUAT (BARBELL)

Position the bar on the rack level with the middle of your chest. Hold the bar with hands just wider than shoulder-width. Step up to the bar and lower yourself until the bar is level with and touching the top of your chest just in front of your shoulders. Without letting go of the bar, bring your elbows forwards and up as high as you can. Keep your elbows as high as possible throughout the lift.
Staying in this position pick the bar up off of the rack and assume a normal squatting stance. Slowly squat down until your quads are parallel to the floor at a minimum, but I suggest you go as low as possible to maximize your range of motion here. Slowly push with your legs and bring the weight back up. Keep your chest up, back straight, and your eyes forward thought the entire lift. Repeat processes until exhaustion or reps are met.

ROMANIAN DEADLIFT (BARBELL)

Standing with your feet together and knees slightly bent, bend over at the waist and grab the bar with your hands just outside your legs. Keep your butt up and your back aligned (see image left). Lift the bar by drawing power from your hamstrings and standing up straight. Keep the bar close to your legs during the lift. Lower the bar back down to the ground in a controlled manner. **Repeat processes until exhaustion or reps are met.**

BARBELL PLATE CALF RAISES

Standing with a barbell on your back, legs together and heels hanging off of a 2-3 inch high platform (you can use a weight plate for this), slowly lower your heels to the ground and back up again. You should pause for one second at the halfway point of each rep. Repeat processes until exhaustion or reps are met.

HANGING LEG RAISES

Hanging from a bar with your arms and legs fully extended, slowly curl your legs up and bring your knees as close to your chest as you can. Keep your core tight and engaged the entire time. Repeat processes until exhaustion or reps are met.

CRUNCHES

Lay down, sit back up.

Keep your core tight, knees bent, and feet flat on the ground the entire time. Repeat processes until exhaustion or reps are met.

ABDOMINAL TWIST

Sitting on your butt, legs partially extended, feet flat on the ground and leaning back approximately 45°, grab a dumbbell or a plate and twist your body from side to side moving only with your core. Count reps for each side. Keep your core tight and engaged the entire time. Repeat processes until exhaustion or reps are met.

7 DIET ASSIGNED

I apologize in advance for having to read this. I know diet will be the least favorite part of this book for a lot of people. No one wants to be told to eat better and clean up their diet. (Well that's too bad. Suck it up, eat better and clean up your diet. Apology redacted.)

Cleaning up your diet and eating better doesn't mean giving up the things you love. It may mean putting the fork down and walking away from the table more often, but not complete abstinence. To do this, I'm going to teach you how to count/track your macros and not hate yourself while dieting.

In a flash, tracking your macros means having a broad idea of what your calorie intake should be and then strategically dividing them up between carbs, fats, and protein to maximize muscle feeding and body composition. There will be two ways to track them, one being better than the other, and one being not as good, but still okay, and much easier if you're strained for time... or just lazy. We'll refer to them as "The More Better Way" and "The Not More Better way".

First, we need to figure out our BMR, and TDEE. I'll list the formulas down below and an area for you to actually write yours in this book.

BMR is calculated differently for males and females. The formulas also vary slightly across the web. The one I'm giving you is pretty standard. If you don't feel like doing all of this work, feel free to go to my website and use the BMR calculator at *www.mencanblog.com.*

BMR Male = 88.362 + (13.397 x weight in kg) + (4.799 x height in cm) – (5.677 x age in years)

BMR Female = 447.593 + (9.247 x weight in kg) + (3.098 x height in cm) – (4.330 x age in years)

Example: 30 years old 200 lbs. (90.7185 kg.) 6 foot (182.88 cm) male:

*88.362 + (13.397 x **90.7185**) + (4.799 x **182.88**) – (5.677 x **30**)*

*(**13.397 x 90.7185**) = 1,215.35574*
*(**4.799 x 182.88**) = 877.64112*
*(**5.677 x 30**) = 170.31*

*88.362 + 1,215.35574 + 877.64112 - 170.31 = **2,011** (**calories rounded**)*

TDEE is just BMR multiplied by an activity level. I have provided you with 2 multipliers, *slightly active,* and *active.* If you're just starting, use *slightly.* If you've been working out for a while already and do your cardio, use *active*.

TDEE = BMR x (activity multiplier)

Multipliers

Slightly active (2-3 days of exercise)	1.375
Active (4-5 days of exercise)	1.55

Example: TDEE for the slightly active 200 lbs. male mentioned earlier
2,011 x 1.375 = 2,765 (calories rounded)

Fill yours in here...

Your BMR:	
Your TDEE:	

Now What?

Now that you've done all of that stupid math, what do you do with it? From here we're going to use the rule of 500 to find our calorie parameters. If you want to bulk increase your TDEE by 500 calories. If you want to cut, subtract 500 calories from your TDEE. If you want to maintain and recomp just stick to your TDEE.

MACROs Done The More Better Way

Now is when MACROs come into play. Take your calories and plug them into these macros formulas.

Bulking:	30% Protein	50% Carbs	20% Fat
Cutting:	40% Protein	40% Carbs	20% fat
Maintaining:	25% Protein	50% Carbs	25% Fat

Our 200 lbs. male, BMR of 2,011 on a slightly active multiplier of 1.374, leaves us with a TDEE of 2,765. He wants to cut, so subtract 500 calories, and you get 2,265 calories. Plug that into the cutting macros, 40% for protein is 906 calories, 40% for carbs is 906 calories, and 20% for fats is 453 calories.

Now you just have to turn those calories into grams. As a reminder 4 calories per gram of protein, 4 calories per gram of carbohydrate, and 9 calories per gram of fat.

Protein   906 / 4 = 226 grams of protein

Carbs   906 / 4 = 226 grams of carbs

Fats   453 / 9 = 50 (rounded) grams of fat

This means this person should be eating 226g protein, 226g carbs, and 50g fat per day. This breakdown and the ratio of macronutrients will ensure your muscles are fed and maintained as well as possible while you're in a caloric defect, or make sure you gain muscle and as little fat as possible if you're bulking.

Macros Done The NOT More Better Way

Decide whether you want to bulk, cut, or maintain, figure those calories using the rule of 500, and figure out the protein intake for that macro. That's it. All you're going to do is make sure you're eating the required about of protein, and staying within your calories.

Example: Same 200 lbs. man wants to cut. He will eat the same 2,265 calories per day, but only track the 226g of protein. The remaining 1,359 calories will be freely eaten from whatever macro source he wants.

Fill yours in here...

Calories	Protein	Carbs	Fats

How Do I Keep Track Of My Macros?

Well, there's an app for that. I use MyFitnessPal to track my macros. The app is super user-friendly and offers all the features we need right there on their free version.

After you calculate your macro breakdown, open MyFitnessPal, and click on *MORE → Goals → Calorie, Carbs, Protein, and Fat Goals*. Once you're there you'll be able to enter your calories and change your percentages to what we already have calculated.

With all of your Macro information plugged into MyFitnessPal, all you have to do now is add food to your diary as you eat it, and let the app do the rest for you. To add food to your diary go to the home screen and start by clicking the blue "+" → FOOD → Meal → Search.

Now just search for the food you want, adjust the amount you're eating, then click the checkmark in the upper right-hand corner. They have a large database of nearly every food available, including most chain restaurants. If they don't have what you're looking for, you can manually enter the information.

Back on the home screen, you will see that it keeps track of everything you've eaten and what you have remaining. You can click on *Diary* for a more detailed breakdown of your macro intake.

Foods

So long as you're hitting all of your numbers, you can eat whatever you want. If you're having a craving for ice cream, fit it into your macros and go have your ice cream. The cleaner the better, but sometimes you just need a clutch cream run, bro.

Meal Times

Eat whenever you want, divided up however you want. The only meal times and portions I will assign to you are pre and post-workout. These numbers are designed to give you adequate energy while training and proper nutrition to feed what you're tearing.

Training on an empty stomach is not advised and can negatively affect your workout and results.

Pre Workout Calories

Protein	**30 grams**
Carbs	**30 grams**
Fat	**As low as possible**

Post Workout Calories

Protein	**40-50 grams**
Carbs	**40-50 grams**
Fat	**Doesn't matter**

Monitoring Results

I only want you to lose or gain 1-2 pounds per week (preferably only 1-1.5). This pace is so you're not cutting so fast that you're sacrificing your muscles, or bulking so fast that you're gaining too much body fat.

You're not going to count your weight change during the

first week. A new diet can do crazy things to your water weight, so we'll start the count at the end of week 2 to give our bodies enough time to adjust. For that same reason, I suggest you don't cheat or reefed the first week either.

I will have a spot for you to track your weight in the last chapter of this book. If you don't see a change in weight by the end of week 2, you have two options. 1. Increase or decrease your cardio, or 2. Increase or decrease your carbs by 25g (100 calories). Keep doing this every week until you see a change on the scale and then stick with that.

Plateau

In a few months, you may hit a plateau and stop seeing the scale move for a few weeks. Probably around the 3-4 month mark. Ask yourself, am I being lazy in my workouts or diet? Forgetting to refeed or cheap? Too much/not enough cardio? If the answer is yes, straighten that crap up and get back to work. If that answer is no, all this means is that your weight has changed so much, that your original TDEE calculation is no longer enough. If you're following the program properly, you've potentially changed in weight by 16-32 lbs.

All you have to do is redo your BMR, TDEE, and Macros calculations. If you want to be lazy, you can just +/- 100 calories worth of carbs (25 carbs) from your diet and try that for a few weeks. Note, your calorie intake should never go below your BMR. If it comes close, you should be increasing your activity level, not decreasing calories. It may be time to change your activity multiplier at this point.

8 SUPPLEMENTATION

Supplements are designed to actually supplement what you're not getting from your diet, or maybe something your body no longer produces effectively. When faced with a couple of million options, choosing or knowing what supplements to take can be overwhelming. I'll do my best to break them down so you have a better idea of what you should be taking, and know what not to waste your money on. Let's stick to 3 categories, *take, maybe take,* and *don't need.*

Take

Multivitamin – Most people need a multivitamin because the average diet is lacking in micronutrients. Even the fruits and vegetables we have today are lacking compared to how they used to be. Our soils aren't as rich as they once were, resulting in much less of the good stuff.

I would suggest something called a vitamin pack. Instead of just one pill, it's a packet containing multiple pills to assure you're getting everything you need. There is normally something for gut health, joint health, heart health, and more all in one convenient pack.

Vitamin C – As we saw in 2019 forward, having a strong immune system can make a large difference in our comfort of life. Your body cannot make or store vitamin C, so getting it from food or supplementation is a necessity daily.

Zinc – Improves immune system and metabolism function. Zinc is also important for wound healing Combined with vitamin C, it makes for an immune system powerhouse.

Vitamin D – Our bodies can make vitamin D using sunlight, but with modern-day indoor jobs and lifestyles, nearly 1/3 of the United States population is D deficient[7]. Vitamin D is utilized for bone density and cellular function across the whole body.

Fish Oil – The magic pill for your joints. Being full of omega fatty acids it's also great for heart health, and your good cholesterol.

Maybe Take

Protein Powder – If you're getting enough from your food, then you won't need protein powder. Pay no mind to the claims you'll hear in the gym like fast-absorbing and slow-digesting proteins. Some of those are true statements, but we are going to keep it simple. Calories are calories and protein is protein.

I know of multiple professionals who don't use it, but also many who do. It's just a personal preference. I personally keep some around for convenience and quick meals. Stick with basic whey powder, with as few carbs and fats as possible.

Creatine – Already discussed at length. Good for muscle building, but not necessary. I recommend it to everyone but not everyone wants another supplement to take.

Sleep Aid – If you're not sleeping a minimum of 6 hours per night, you may look into this. If you're not waking up feeling well-rested with enough energy to get through the day, you may look into this. Do you feel like you sleep fine? If ain't broke, don't fix it.

Digestive Support – A lot of people have stomach issues when they start eating real whole foods. Probiotics or digestive enzymes can help with this. Even if your stomach is fine, the "good bacteria" these supplements offer can have multiple health benefits as well for general wellness and immune support.

Powdered Greens – I don't eat a veggie-heavy diet regularly. I know that plants still offer awesome nutritional benefits, so I choose to just take a powdered greens supplement every day. It's just another way of getting in the vital vitamins and minerals.

Electrolytes – While drinking water alone will keep you hydrated, we're still pushing out a lot of electrolytes when we sweat. If you're going to sauna or pick one of the higher intensity cardio options, you may look into this. If you're not a heavy sweater and chose a lighter cardio option, water alone may be fine for you.

Don't Need

Pre Workout – These are supplements full of caffeine, nitric oxide booster, and other simulants that you take before a workout. They're designed to get you moving and get your blood pumping. They are positively awesome, but not "needed" if you're on a tight budget.

If you're new to this and want to dabble your toes in the world of pre-workouts, start by taking them on days you work larger muscle groups, like leg or back day.

Amino Acids – I hope your diet is going to be well round enough not to need these. Besides, there isn't a lot of evidence showing that your body is absorbing enough amino acids from supplementation to make a difference.

Meal Replacement Shakes and Carb Powders – Whenever possible, we want to eat our calories as opposed to drinking them. Keeping some around for a quick convenience is okay, but these powders can be expensive and still struggle with the quality of ingredients. It's not necessary.

Mass gainers – Same deal as above. If you're serious about gaining mass, pick up a freaking fork, and stop looking for answers inside expensive powders. Food is our friend.

Over The Counter Muscle Builders – These pills are packed full of empty promises and garbage. If they worked everyone would be doing it and walking around completely sauced. Calories, hypertrophy, rest, done.

Over The Counter Testosterone Boosters – These again are full of empty promises. The effects they have on your testosterone are minimal to none and definitely not enough to entertain the cost. Expensive and does not work as advertised, ask me how I know.

If you feel like you have low testosterone, go ask your doctor to check your levels, and maybe consult a specialist in that field. If you're in your 30s consider getting this checked even if you feel fine, as this is around the age levels start going down naturally and you'll want a baseline to go off of later.

9 YOU'RE SO EXTRA

Have you ever seen a dude in the gym with a thick leather belt strapped across his gut way too tight and thought to yourself "Wow bro, you're so extra"? There are probably a couple of things you've seen and thought that about. Let's talk about what all of these extras are and what they're used for. You may decide you need some of them, so check my website *www.mencanblog.com* for their links.

Lifting belt – The thick leather belt mentioned above. Worn more so across the core than the waist. Normally only utilized on larger lifts when the weight gets heavy, but some people will still wear it on heavy sets of smaller muscle groups. Used to stabilize the spine and maintain abdominal pressure during lifting.

Lifting Straps – Normally woven nylon, or leather, these are straps that wrap around your wrist, and then around the barbell to help you hold on to heavy weights.

Wrist Straps – Elastic straps that wrap around your wrist multiple times. Works to stabilize and brace the wrist.

Chalk – Gym chalk is just white chalk that you rub on your hands to keep them from sweating. Used for bettering grip.

Knee Sleeves – Thick compression sleeves that go over your knees to stabilize, brace and compress them. Helps when recovering front an injury or hitting really heavy weights.

Elbow Sleeves – Believe it or not... a thick compression sleeve that goes over your elbow to stabilize, brace, and compress it. Helps when recovering front an injury or hitting really heavy weights.

Lifting Shoes – These are more than just a pair of gym shoes with ankle support. These were originally built for collegiate and professional lifters/competitions. Designed so lifters can maintain a proper posture and stable platform when lifting. You'll recognize them by their distinctive dad-style Velcro tops and thick tall heels.

Mouthpieces – Some people tend to grind and press on their teeth when lifting large amounts of weight, so these were made to mitigate some of that. Some interesting studies discuss how a mouthpiece can better align your jaw with your head and neck allowing you to lift heavier, but that's for another time.

Gloves – These are just gloves for covering your soft, delicate, pretty hands. Some people are afraid of the calluses that lifting weights will bring you, some people embrace it.

Smelling Salts – This is a container of granulated ammonia that when inhaled, sends a shiver of mixed emotions throughout your whole body and makes you want to lift everything. It is a fast rush and not a prolonged feeling at all. You'll see people use them right before a lift. It should be noted that you are only inhaling the fumes, not the actual substance. I've never really understood these and they're not super common, but better you hear it here first.

10 SHOPPING LIST

Getting your macros in and watching your calories can be challenging at first, so I have a list of each macronutrient for you to give you some ideas on what you can eat to help you meet your food goals.

A handy rule to remember, the cleaner the better. For example, you will see popcorn on the carbs list. You will want to choose the popcorn with the least amount of fat and the least amount of ingredients to assure the cleanest form possible. Another example is peanut butter. You need the all-natural no sugar added peanut butter with the only ingredients being peanuts and salt.

If you're going with the cutting diet, volume is going to be your friend. As an example, you can have 6 cups of low-fat popcorn for the same amount of calories as 1 cup of white rice. Another tool for your belt, making a blended protein and fruit smoothing and throwing a few handfuls of ice in there.

Carbs	Cals	Pro	Carb	Fat
Oats	150	5g	27g	3g
Cream of rice	160	3g	36g	0g
Brown Rice	160	4g	35g	1g
White rice	160	3g	36g	0g
Quinoa	170	6g	29g	2.5g
Lentils	150	12g	25g	.5g
Russet potatoes	110	3g	26g	0g
Sweet potatoes	110	3g	26g	0g
Squash Plants	50	2g	14g	0g
Plain Rice cakes	35	1g	7g	0g
Rice milk	130	0g	27g	2.5g
Ezekiel bread	80	5g	15g	.5g
Brown rice noodles	200	4g	45g	1g
Black Beans	110	7g	20g	0g
Honey	60	0g	17g	0g
Agave Nectar	60	0g	17g	0g
Banana	105	1g	27g	0g
Strawberries	45	1g	11g	0g
Grapes	90	0g	23g	0g
Apple	95	0g	25g	0g
Blueberries	80	1g	20g	0g
Pop Corn (Low Fat)	160	3g	28g	6g

Protein	Cals	Pro	Carb	Fat
White Chicken	120	26g	0g	2g
Dark Chicken	160	21g	0g	8g
Turkey Breast	120	28g	0g	.5g
Lean Beef 97/3	130	24g	0g	4g
Lean Bison 90/10	200	24g	0g	11g
Lean Pork	120	23g	0g	2.5g
Cod Fish	90	20g	0g	1g
Tuna	120	30g	0g	1g
Salmon	270	35g	0g	14g
Shrimp	80	15g	1g	1g
Tofu	70	7g	2g	4g
Whole Eggs	72	6g	0g	5g
Egg Whites	16	4g	0g	0g
Whey Protein	120	25g	3g	0g
Skim Milk	80	8g	11g	0g
Greek Yogurt	100	18g	8	0g

Fat	Cals	Pro	Carb	Fat
Almonds	170	6g	6g	15g
Peanut Butter	190	7g	8g	14g
Grass-Fed Butter	100	0g	0g	12g
Avocado	80	1g	4g	8g
Healthy Oils	120	0g	0g	14g

Zero Calorie Items
Water (Ice)
Coffee/Tea
Vinegar
Flavor Extracts
Herbs and Spices
Diet Soda
Mustard
Hot Sauce
Stevia
Lemons/Limes

11 THE OUTRO

Below are some important key takeaways from this book to summarize everything we've talked about.

• Your doctor knows more than I do and their advisement is far superior to mine.

• This is a progressive muscle overload program.

• This program uses compound lifting exercises. You don't need fancy machines, just dumbbells, and barbells.

• You can't be too busy for your health. There is a 3-day option for even the busiest people in the world. Find the time to buy the time.

• Calories in vs. calories out. Don't overcomplicate it.

• Cardio hates you but you need it.

• Recovery/rest should have your full undivided attention.

• Grown men shouldn't eat plain cheese pizza.

• Diet sodas and sugar replacements are not the devil.

• Diets don't have to make you hate yourself. Using macros allows you to have the foods you love.

• You should probably take a few supplements that make sense for you.

• It's okay to be a little extra, but not too extra.

• Don't order hot chocolate in a coffee shop.

• Having More Muscle is More Better.

12 TRACKING

You did it. The end of a really good, super great, awesome book. I've provided you with enough tracking sheets for 10 weeks of each exercise described in this book. If you run out or just want a more visit my website *www.mencanblog.com* and click on the *More Muscle More Better* page. You will find links to all my books and tracking journals.

Now, stop reading and go workout.

Starting Weight

Date	Weight

Weight Tracking

Week	Date	Weight
End of Week 1	*Omit*	*Omit*
End of Week 2		
End of Week 3		
End of Week 4		
End of Week 5		
End of Week 6		
End of Week 7		
End of Week 8		
End of Week 9		
End of Week 10		

Macro References For Future usage

Date:

Calories	Protein	Carbs	Fats

Date:

Calories	Protein	Carbs	Fats

Date:

Calories	Protein	Carbs	Fats

Example Sheet:

EXERCISE: Flat Bench Press				
DATE	**WEIGHT**	**SET 1**	**SET 2**	**SET 3**
01-01-22	225	7	6	6
01-08-22	225	7	7	6
01-15-22	225	8	6	6
01-22-22	225	8	7	7
01-29-22	225	8	8	8
02-05-22	235	6	6	7

NOTES :

Hit 8 reps for 3 sets in a row on 01/29. will be moving up next week!

Weight increase by 10 lbs. on 02/05. Felt good, need to slow my reps down

EXERCISE:_____

DATE	WEIGHT	SET 1	SET 2	SET 3

NOTES :

EXERCISE:_____

DATE	WEIGHT	SET 1	SET 2	SET 3

NOTES :

_____

_____

_____

_____

_____

_____

_____

_____

_____

EXERCISE:_____

DATE	WEIGHT	SET 1	SET 2	SET 3

NOTES :

_____

_____

_____

_____

_____

_____

_____

_____

_____

EXERCISE:_____

DATE	WEIGHT	SET 1	SET 2	SET 3

NOTES :

_____

_____

_____

_____

_____

_____

_____

_____

_____

EXERCISE:_____

DATE	WEIGHT	SET 1	SET 2	SET 3

NOTES :

EXERCISE:_____

DATE	WEIGHT	SET 1	SET 2	SET 3

NOTES :

_____

_____

_____

_____

_____

_____

_____

_____

EXERCISE: _____

DATE	WEIGHT	SET 1	SET 2	SET 3

NOTES :

_____

_____

_____

_____

_____

_____

_____

_____

_____

EXERCISE:_____

DATE	WEIGHT	SET 1	SET 2	SET 3

NOTES :

EXERCISE:_____

DATE	WEIGHT	SET 1	SET 2	SET 3

NOTES :

EXERCISE:_____

DATE	WEIGHT	SET 1	SET 2	SET 3

NOTES :

EXERCISE:_____

DATE	WEIGHT	SET 1	SET 2	SET 3

NOTES :

EXERCISE:_____

DATE	WEIGHT	SET 1	SET 2	SET 3

NOTES :

EXERCISE:_____

DATE	WEIGHT	SET 1	SET 2	SET 3

NOTES :

EXERCISE:_____

DATE	WEIGHT	SET 1	SET 2	SET 3

NOTES :

EXERCISE:_____

DATE	WEIGHT	SET 1	SET 2	SET 3

NOTES :

_____
_____
_____
_____
_____
_____
_____
_____
_____

EXERCISE:_____

DATE	WEIGHT	SET 1	SET 2	SET 3

NOTES :

EXERCISE:_____

DATE	WEIGHT	SET 1	SET 2	SET 3

NOTES :

_____
_____
_____
_____
_____
_____
_____
_____
_____

EXERCISE:_____

DATE	WEIGHT	SET 1	SET 2	SET 3

NOTES :

EXERCISE:_____

DATE	WEIGHT	SET 1	SET 2	SET 3

NOTES :

EXERCISE:_____

DATE	WEIGHT	SET 1	SET 2	SET 3

NOTES :

_____

_____

_____

_____

_____

_____

_____

_____

EXERCISE:_____

DATE	WEIGHT	SET 1	SET 2	SET 3

NOTES :

EXERCISE:_____

DATE	WEIGHT	SET 1	SET 2	SET 3

NOTES :

EXERCISE:_____

DATE	WEIGHT	SET 1	SET 2	SET 3

NOTES :

_____

_____

_____

_____

_____

_____

_____

_____

_____

SOURCES

1. Tey SL, Salleh NB, Henry J, Forde CG. Effects of aspartame-, monk fruit-, stevia- and sucrose-sweetened beverages on postprandial glucose, insulin, and energy intake. Int J Obes (Lond). 2017 Mar;41(3):450-457. doi: 10.1038/ijo.2016.225. Epub 2016 Dec 13. PMID: 27956737.

2. Ahmad SY, Friel J, Mackay D. The Effects of Non-Nutritive Artificial Sweeteners, Aspartame and Sucralose, on the Gut Microbiome in Healthy Adults: Secondary Outcomes of a Randomized Double-Blinded Crossover Clinical Trial. Nutrients. 2020 Nov 6;12(11):3408. doi: 10.3390/nu12113408. PMID: 33171964; PMCID: PMC7694690.

3. Kim Y, Keogh JB, Clifton PM. Consumption of a Beverage Containing Aspartame and Acesulfame K for Two Weeks Does Not Adversely Influence Glucose Metabolism in Adult Males and Females: A Randomized Crossover Study. Int J Environ Res Public Health. 2020 Dec 4;17(23):9049. doi: 10.3390/ijerph17239049. PMID: 33291649; PMCID: PMC7731387.

4. Kim HJ, Kim CK, Carpentier A, Poortmans JR. Studies on the safety of creatine supplementation. Amino Acids. 2011 May;40(5):1409-18. doi: 10.1007/s00726-011-0878-2. Epub 2011 Mar 12. PMID: 21399917.

5. Kay AD, Blazevich AJ. Effect of acute static stretch on maximal muscle performance: a systematic review. Med Sci Sports Exerc. 2012 Jan;44(1):154-64. doi: 10.1249/MSS.0b013e318225cb27. PMID: 21659901.

6. Schoenfeld BJ, Aragon A, Wilborn C, Urbina SL, Hayward SE, Krieger J. Pre- versus post-exercise protein intake has similar effects on muscular adaptations. PeerJ. 2017 Jan 3;5:e2825. doi: 10.7717/peerj.2825. Erratum in: PeerJ. 2017 Aug 1;5: PMID: 28070459; PMCID: PMC5214805.

7. Centers for Disease Control and Prevention. (2022, February 1). *Micronutrient facts.* Centers for Disease Control and Prevention. Retrieved May 17, 2022, from https://www.cdc.gov/nutrition/micronutrient-malnutrition/micronutrients/index.html

8. Moreira JBN, Wohlwend M, Wisløff U. Exercise and cardiac health: physiological and molecular insights. Nat Metab. 2020 Sep;2(9):829-839. doi: 10.1038/s42255-020-0262-1. Epub 2020 Aug 17. PMID: 32807982.

9. Obadike, Obi. "How Much Cardio Is Too Much?" *Bodybuilding.com*, 11 Dec. 2018, https://www.bodybuilding.com/content/ask-the-ripped-dude-how-much-cardio-is-too-much.html#:~:text=Actually%2C%20performing%20too%20much%20ocardio,a%20tough%20time%20burning%20fat.

10. Wallis GA, Gonzalez JT. Is exercise best served on an empty stomach? Proc Nutr Soc. 2019 Feb;78(1):110-117. doi: 10.1017/S0029665118002574. Epub 2018 Oct 18. PMID: 30334499.

11. Patrick RP, Johnson TL. Sauna use as a lifestyle practice to extend healthspan. Exp Gerontol. 2021 Oct 15;154:111509. doi: 10.1016/j.exger.2021.111509. Epub 2021 Aug 5. PMID: 34363927.

12. Laukkanen JA, Laukkanen T, Kunutsor SK. Cardiovascular and Other Health Benefits of Sauna Bathing: A Review of the Evidence. Mayo Clin Proc. 2018 Aug;93(8):1111-1121.doi: 10.1016/j.mayocp.2018.04.008. PMID: 30077204.

13. Miwa T, Chadani Y, Taguchi H. Escherichia coli small heat shock protein IbpA is an aggregation-sensor that self-regulates its own expression at posttranscriptional levels. Mol Microbiol. 2021 Jan;115(1):142-156. doi: 10.1111/mmi.14606. Epub 2020 Oct 14. PMID: 32959419.

14. Singh DP, Barani Lonbani Z, Woodruff MA, Parker TJ, Steck R, Peake JM. Effects of Topical Icing on Inflammation, Angiogenesis, Revascularization, and Myofiber Regeneration in Skeletal Muscle Following Contusion Injury. Front Physiol. 2017 Mar 7;8:93. doi: 10.3389/fphys.2017.00093. PMID: 28326040; PMCID: PMC5339266.

15. Malanga GA, Yan N, Stark J. Mechanisms and efficacy of heat and cold therapies for musculoskeletal injury. Postgrad Med. 2015 Jan;127(1):57-65. doi: 10.1080/00325481.2015.992719. Epub 2014 Dec 15. PMID: 25526231.

16. Seguin R, Nelson ME. The benefits of strength training for older adults. Am J Prev Med. 2003 Oct;25(3 Suppl 2):141-9. doi: 10.1016/s0749-3797(03)00177-6. PMID: 14552938.

17. "Alcohol Beverage Labeling." *TTBGov - Alcohol Beverage Labeling*, https://www.ttb.gov/labeling-wine/alcohol-beverage-labeling

18. Zakhari S. Overview: how is alcohol metabolized by the body? Alcohol Res Health. 2006;29(4):245-54. PMID: 17718403; PMCID: PMC6527027.

19. Hosker DK, Elkins RM, Potter MP. Promoting Mental Health and Wellness in Youth Through Physical Activity, Nutrition, and Sleep. Child Adolesc Psychiatr Clin N Am. 2019 Apr;28(2):171-193. doi: 10.1016/j.chc.2018.11.010. Epub 2019 Feb 6. PMID: 30832951.

20. Zwerling B, Keymeulen S, Krychman ML. Sleep and Sex: A Review of the Interrelationship of Sleep and Sexuality Disorders in the Female Population, Through the Lens of Sleeping Beauty Syndrome. Sex Med Rev. 2021 Apr;9(2):221-229. doi: 10.1016/j.sxmr.2020.08.005. Epub 2020 Oct 3. PMID: 33023862.

Rights and license to use photos/illustrations were purchased from
https://www.gymvisual.com/

Printed in Great Britain
by Amazon

46100868R00079